Christmas Traditions around the World

by Ann Ingalls • illustrated by Elisa Chavarri

Published by The Child's World®
1980 Lookout Drive • Mankato, MN 56003-1705
800-599-READ • www.childsworld.com

Acknowledgments
The Child's World®: Mary Berendes, Publishing Director
Red Line Editorial: Editorial direction
The Design Lab: Design
Amnet: Production

Design elements: Ilaszlo/Shutterstock Images

Photographs ©: Wojciech Gajda/iStockphoto, cover, title page;
Zvonimir Atletic/Shutterstock Images, 5; Shutterstock Images, 9, 17; Lisa
Tannenbaum/iStockphoto, 11; Jan Kranendonk/Shutterstock Images, 13;
Alexander Hoffmann/Shutterstock Images, 16; Dimitrios/Shutterstock
Images, 21; Richard Gunion/iStockphoto, 25; Kuttelvaserova/Shutterstock
Images, 29

ISBN 9781614734253
LCCN 2012946510

Printed in the United States of America
Mankato, MN
April, 2014
PA02229

Dedication
For Martha Rolf, who celebrates life so beautifully

About the Author

Ann Ingalls's first book, *The Little Piano Girl*, was published by Houghton Mifflin in January 2010. Pilgrim Press released her second book, *Worm Watching and Other Wonderful Ways to Teach Young Children to Pray*, in May 2012. Her first emergent reader, *Ice Cream Soup*, will hit shelves in June 2013. Visit Ann at www.anningallswrites.com.

About the Illustrator

Elisa Chavarri is a Peruvian illustrator who works from her home in Alpena, Michigan, which she shares with her husband, Matt, and her cat, Sergeant Tibbs. She has previously illustrated *Fly Blanky Fly*, by Anne Margaret Lewis, and *Fairly Fairy Tales*, by Esmé Raji Codell.

Table of Contents

Chapter One

The Christmas Story

Christmas is on December 25 every year. Many people all around the world **celebrate**. Each country celebrates the holiday in its own way. Some people even celebrate on a different day.

Christmas began as a celebration of the birth of Jesus Christ. Christians believe Jesus is the son of God. The Christian Bible says Jesus was born about 2,000 years ago. No one knows for sure if December 25 is the day Jesus was born.

People tell the story of Jesus's birth at Christmas. An angel visited Jesus's mother, Mary. The angel said she would have a child. The child would be God's son.

Soon, the government said it wanted to count all the people. Everyone had to travel to the city where he or she was born. Mary traveled miles from Nazareth to Bethlehem. These cities are in or near the modern country of Israel. She went with her husband Joseph.

Mary and Joseph looked for somewhere to stay in Bethlehem. Many stories say Jesus was born in a stable. **Shepherds** came to see the baby. They knew he was special. Three wise kings came. They brought presents for Jesus. Jesus grew up and brought his message of peace and love to the world.

This stained glass window shows Jesus's birth.

Chapter Two

Santa Claus

People around the world tell stories about Santa Claus. Santa Claus is a jolly old man. He has a long white beard and wears red clothes. He brings presents to good boys and girls on Christmas Eve. Christmas Eve is December 24. That is the evening before Christmas Day.

Santa Claus lives at the North Pole with his wife, Mrs. Claus. His elf friends help him make Christmas presents all year. On Christmas Eve, he loads presents in his sleigh. Flying reindeer pull the sleigh.

Santa and his reindeer fly all around the world. They land on rooftops. Santa goes down the chimney. He leaves Christmas presents in stockings and under the Christmas tree. Children leave Santa a snack of milk and cookies. Sometimes, they leave carrots for his reindeer, too.

Parts of the Santa Claus story go back hundreds of years. They are about Saint Nick, or Saint Nicholas. A baby boy named Nicholas was born in Patara. This village is in the modern country of Turkey. He was born around 300 AD. When he was a small boy, his parents died.

His parents left Nicholas a lot of money. He wanted to help the poor. So, he gave all his money away. Then he started working in the church. He became a bishop. He continued helping people in need. Later he became Saint Nicholas.

Stories about Saint Nicholas grew and changed. People celebrated his life at Christmas time. In the Netherlands, people called him *Sinterklaas* (SIN-ter-class). Later people began to call him Santa Claus.

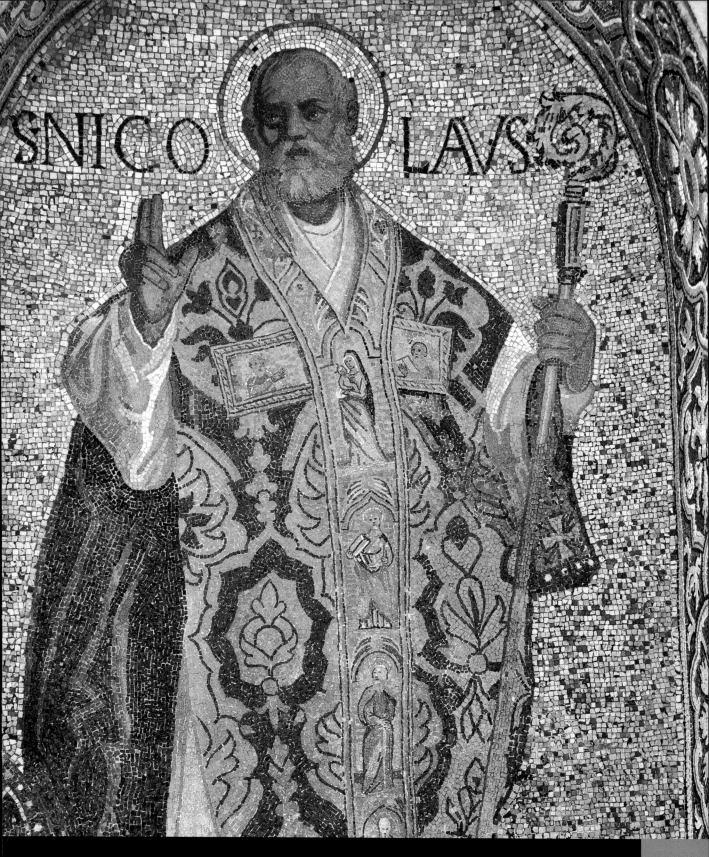

Saint Nicholas was a bishop who helped the poor.

Chapter Three

Christmas in the United States

Americans love to give gifts and send cards at Christmas. They visit with family and friends. Some people go to church on Christmas Eve.

For Christmas dinner, lots of people eat roast turkey, ham, or goose. They eat Christmas cookies, pies, or other desserts.

Holly, **mistletoe**, and **nativity** scenes fill many homes. Many families decorate Christmas trees. They hang lights, tinsel, **ornaments**, strings of popcorn, and candy canes.

Different parts of the United States have their own **traditions** as well. There is a Christmas parade in New Orleans. An ox walks down the street. People decorate its horns with holly and ribbons.

People in New Mexico fill paper bags with sand. They place lit candles inside. The bags are called *luminarias* (loo-meen-AR-ee-ahs). They put the bags on streets and rooftops to light the way for the Christ child.

People in New Mexico light their homes with luminarias.

Chapter Four

Christmas in the Netherlands

In the Netherlands, Santa Claus is called Sinterklaas. *Zwarte Piet* (ZWAR-tah PEET), or Black Peter, is his helper. Sinterklaas arrives in a boat in November. People go to the docks to greet him. Then there is a big parade. He rides a white horse through the streets.

Sinterklaas rides around the country until December 6. He checks if children have been good or bad. Good children get presents. People give more gifts on December 6. At sunset each night during the Christmas season, farmers blow long horns over water.

On Christmas morning, many people go to church. In the afternoon, people sit around the Christmas tree. They sing **carols** and tell stories.

Sinterklaas rides a horse around the Netherlands.

Chapter Five

Christmas in Egypt

Christians in Egypt celebrate Christmas on January 7. They eat no meat for 40 days before the holiday. This time is called *Kiahk* (KEE-ahk). They sing special songs on Saturday nights during Kiahk. Then they go to church on Sunday mornings.

On January 6, Egyptian Christmas Eve, Christians go to a special church service. Everyone eats *qurban* (kur-BAHN) bread. This special bread sometimes has a cross on it. The cross stands for Jesus Christ. Families eat meat and rice together after the service. This meal is called *fatta* (FAH-tah).

On Christmas morning, friends and family gather for parties. Children get a gift called *El 'aidia* (el AY-dee-ah). This is money to buy toys and sweets.

Santa Claus in Egypt is called *Baba Noël* (bah-bah NO-ell). This means "Father Christmas."

Chapter Six

Christmas in Chile

Children in Chile put clay nativity sets under their Christmas trees. The sets are called *pesebre* (peh-SEH-bray). Santa Claus is called *Viejito Pascuero* (vee-ay-HEE-toh pas-KWAYR-oh). He wishes everyone *"feliz navidad y un prospero Año Nuevo."* Merry Christmas and a prosperous New Year!

Chapter Seven

Christmas in China

Only 3 to 4 percent of people in China are Christian. But many more people hang decorations and give presents. In China, Christmas trees are called "trees of light." The trees are usually plastic. Children decorate them with colorful ornaments. The ornaments are made from paper. They are shaped like flowers, chains, and stars.

Santa Claus is called *Sheng Dan Lao Ren*. This means "Christmas Old Man." Sheng Dan Lao Ren has a white beard. He wears a red silk robe. Children hang up stockings for him to put presents in.

Chapter Eight

Christmas in Denmark

On Christmas in Denmark, the family eats dinner and sings carols and **hymns**. People eat roast goose stuffed with prunes. They eat red cabbage and browned potatoes. They eat fried pastries and *risengrod* (RIH-zen-grul). Risengrod is rice pudding with cinnamon. They hide almonds in it. The child who finds one gets a prize.

Danes pile fruit and biscuits on special Christmas plates. They give these to friends and family. They also leave dishes of seed outside to feed the wild birds.

Many Danes believe in an elf named *Nisse* (NIH-suh). Nisse likes children and plays tricks on people. He wears gray clothes, a red bonnet, and white clogs. People leave rice pudding out for Nisse to keep him happy.

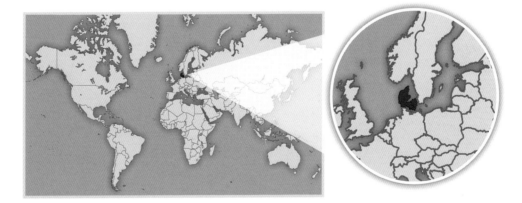

Chapter Nine

Christmas in Greece

Many Greeks tell stories of Saint Nicholas working on the sea. He saves sinking ships and rescues people. His clothes and beard are soaked with salty seawater. Greek sailors do not go out to sea without a picture of Saint Nicholas.

On Christmas Eve, families gather around the holiday table. They eat sweet golden loaves of *christopsomo* (hree-STOHP-shoh-moh), or "Christ bread." The table is filled with nut cookies and figs that were dried on rooftops.

On Christmas Day, small boys and girls go from house to house. They beat drums, play triangles, and sing carols. People give them dried figs, almonds, walnuts, and sweets. People greet one another by saying *xronia polla* (HROW-nya poh-LAH), or "many happy years."

Many Greek families bake nut cookies for Christmas.

Chapter Ten

Christmas in Uganda

Christmas is called *Sekukulu* (SEH-koo-koo-loo) in Uganda. It begins on December 24. People hold a night church service. Churches are decorated. People sing Christmas carols. Women wear dresses in bright colors with matching turbans.

Holiday cooking starts after church. Good smells fill the air. Children sweep the courtyard. They take food to friends and family.

People prepare a special dish called *luwombo* (loo-WOM-boh). Chicken is smoked and wrapped in banana leaves. It is steamed for hours. The bananas give the chicken a wonderful taste.

After Christmas dinner, storytelling, games, dancing, and singing begin. The fun goes on until early the next morning.

Chapter Eleven

Christmas in Mexico

Christmas is called *Navidad* (nah-vee-DAD) in Mexico. In the nine days before Christmas, many Mexicans take part in *las posadas* (lahs poh-SAH-dahs), which means "inns." People dressed as Joseph and Mary knock on doors. They are searching for a place for Jesus to be born. Homeowners welcome them inside.

Inside, a party waits. Everyone eats and sings. Children hit a piñata. They munch on cookies called *biscochitos* (bees-coh-CHEE-tohs). Families set up *nacimientos* (nah-see-mee-EN-tohs), or nativity scenes.

On Christmas Day, families spend time together. They go to church and then they eat a special meal. Some families eat turkey. Others eat *menudo* (meh-NOO-doh), a beef stew, or *tamales* (tah-MAH-leys), corn filling cooked in a wrapper.

Children get presents on January 6. This is the feast of *los reyes magos* (lohs RAY-ehs MAH-gohs), the three wise kings who brought Jesus presents. Children put their shoes near a window so the kings can fill them with candy and small gifts.

Mexican children break piñatas at Christmas time.

Chapter Twelve

Christmas in India

People in India speak many different languages. They have many names for Santa Claus, too. Some names are Baba Christmas, Christmas *Thaathaa* (tah-TAH), and *Natal Bua* (nah-TAH BOO-ah). Santa Claus brings presents in a horse-drawn cart.

Many Christians in India decorate mango or banana trees. In some places, people put small clay lamps outside. They put them on the flat roofs of their houses.

On Christmas Eve, people buy presents and new clothes. At midnight, families go to church together. On Christmas Day, they eat a special meal. They eat yellow rice and pastries dyed red and pink. They also eat a kind of Christmas fruitcake.

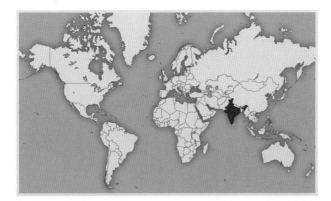

People around the world sing songs about Christmas and Santa Claus. This Dutch song is sung in the Netherlands.

Hoor de Wind Waait
Door de Bomen

Hoor de wind waait door de bomen
hier in huis daar waait de wind.
Zou de goede Sint wel komen,
nu hij het weer zo lelijk vindt?
Nu hij het weer zo lelijk vindt.
Als hij komt in donkere nachten,
op zijn paardje o zo snel.
Als hij wist hoe zeer wij wachten,
ja gewis dan kwam hij wel,
ja gewis dan kwam hij wel.

(in English)
Listen How the Wind Blows through the Trees

Listen how the wind blows through the trees
even here in the house the wind is blowing.
You think Santa Claus is still coming,
since the weather is so nasty?
Since the weather is so nasty.
He travels in dark nights,
on his horsey, oh so fast.
If he knew how much we long to see him,
then for sure he will come,
then for sure he will come.

Hands-On

Eating special foods is part of Christmas in many cultures. Ask an adult to help you make this Christmas bread from Chile.

Christmas Bread from Chile

Ingredients

butter or non-stick cooking spray for the baking pan
2 cups (284 g) self-rising flour
1 cup (142 g) plain flour
1 teaspoon baking powder
1 stick butter
1 cup (198 g) sugar
2 eggs
1 teaspoon (5 ml) vanilla
1 cup (237 ml) milk
1 cup (226 g) sultanas and chopped almonds (mixed)
½ cup (113 g) candied fruit
grated rind of 1 lemon
½ cup (113 g) glazed cherries

Directions

1. Preheat the oven to 350 degrees Fahrenheit (177°C). Grease or butter an 8 inch by 8 inch (20 cm by 20 cm) square baking pan.
2. In a medium bowl, sift together the self-rising flour, the plain flour, and the baking powder.
3. In a large bowl, cut butter into pieces.
4. Add sugar to butter and mix until creamy. Add eggs, vanilla, and milk and mix well.
5. Add the flour mixture into the butter mixture and stir together.
6. Add sultanas and almonds, candied fruit, lemon rind, and cherries to flour.
7. Mix well and pour into the prepared baking pan.
8. Bake at 350 degrees for about 1 ½ hours or until a toothpick inserted into the loaf comes out clean.

Glossary

carols (KAR-uhls) Carols are joyful Christmas songs or hymns. The children sang Christmas carols.

celebrate (SEL-uh-brate) To celebrate is to observe or take notice of a special day. Many people celebrate Christmas.

holly (HAH-lee) Holly is a tree or shrub with glossy leaves, red berries and white flowers. Some people put up holly at Christmas.

hymns (HIMS) Hymns are religious songs. People sing hymns on Christmas.

mistletoe (MIS-uhl-toh) Mistletoe is a plant with yellow flowers and white berries. People put up mistletoe at Christmas.

nativity (nuh-TIV-i-tee) A nativity is a scene with figures (usually dolls or statues) that represent Jesus's birth. People put out nativity scenes.

ornament (OR-nuh-munt) An ornament is an object used to decorate. Please put an ornament on the Christmas tree.

shepherds (SHUP-urds) Shepherds are people who take care of sheep. Shepherds came to visit Jesus after he was born.

traditions (truh-DISH-uns) Traditions are ways of thinking or acting communicated through culture. Many families have Christmas traditions.

Learn More

Books

Hollihan, Kerrie Logan. *Christmas Traditions in Latin America*. New York: PowerKids Press, 2010.

Onyefulu, Ifeoma. *An African Christmas*. London: Frances Lincoln, 2005.

Web Sites

Visit our Web site for links about Christmas traditions around the world: ***childsworld.com/links***

Note to Parents, Teachers, and Librarians: We routinely verify our Web links to make sure they are safe and active sites. So encourage your readers to check them out!

Index